CW01671574

THE CIRCLE OF LIFE

The Circle of Life

Creative Ideas for Primary RE
through Circle Time, Group Activities
and the Liturgical Year

Sister Judith Russi SSMN

Illustrations by Kati Teague

Matthew James Publishing Ltd

First published in 2003 by
Matthew James Publishing Ltd
19 Wellington Close
Chelmsford
Essex CM1 2EE

© 2003 Judith Russi SSMN
Illustrations © 2003 Kati Teague

The right of Judith Russi to be identified as the
author of this work has been asserted in accordance with
the Copyright, Designs and Patents Act 1988

ISBN 1 898366 72 1

Designed by Peter Robb
Printed and bound in Great Britain by J W Arrowsmith, Bristol

Introduction 1
Setting the Scene 4
Ways into the Circle 5
Entering the Circle 6
The Talking Feather .7
New Beginnings 10
Thanksgiving 19
Heroes and Heroines 23
Advent 28
Christmas & Epiphany 36
Candlemas 44
Lent 47
Easter 50
Pentecost 57
Goodbye 60

"May they all be one…"

John 17:11

With particular thanks to all our wonderful teachers in the Archdiocese of Westminster who have contributed to the ideas in this book.

Introduction

Circle Time is well established in many Primary Schools and it is not the aim of this resource to outline the rationale or the mechanics for holding a circle time with your class. What I hope this resource will do is support and help you in your classroom with some well tried and tested ideas for a successful Circle Time in RE.

All of the ideas suggested here have been used in RE. However, they can of course be used outside the dedicated RE slot on the timetable.

An Ancient Tradition

There is nothing new about the concept of the circle and the positive influence that it can have on an individual and a community.

The ritual and practice of gathering in a circle is found in many cultures and civilisations down through the ages.

The cornerstone of Christianity is the never ending circle of the loving relationship between The Father, Son and Holy Spirit. This is beautifully expressed by the Russian Iconologist Andrei Rublev in his famous Icon of the Trinity first painted in the 15th century.

Here Rublev depicts the Trinity, as an indivisible essence, without beginning or end, infinite and eternal.

What we see in this picture is part of a larger Icon painted by Rublev illustrating the story of the three mysterious visitors who come to see Abraham and Sarah.

Genesis 18
"Yahweh appeared to him at the Oak of Mamre while he was sitting by the entrance of the tent during the hottest part of the day. He looked up, and there he saw three men standing near him. As soon as he saw them he ran from the entrance of the tent to greet them, and bowed to the ground. "My lord," he said, "if I find favour with you please do not pass you servant by. Let me have a little water brought, and you can wash your feet and have a rest under the tree. Let me fetch a little bread and you can refresh yourselves before going further, now that you have come in your servant's direction." They replied, "Do as you say."

Abraham hurried to the tent and said to Sarah, "Quick, knead three measures of best flour and make loaves." Then running to the herd, Abraham took a fine and tender calf and gave it to the servant, who hurried to prepare it. Then taking curds, milk and the calf which had been prepared, he laid all before them, and they ate while he remained standing near them under the tree."

Each section of the Icon tells a part of the story. Years 5 and 6 love to work out the meaning behind each part of the Icon.

The three visitors are shown as angels, thus illustrating that they belong to heaven and not to earth. You will notice that their faces are identical. This is to emphasise that each represents the equality of the three Persons of the Holy Trinity. Notice also that they are neither male nor female in their appearance. It is thought that the figure on the left, dressed in almost transparent shades of pale pink with brown and blue-green highlights is God the Father.

Look carefully at his hand. It could be pointing to the meat in the dish, or to the second figure next to him, the Son or the Lamb of God, or in fact it could be that he is holding up one finger to signifying the First Person of the Trinity.

Directly above this angel on the left, is a building which symbolised the Church and worship of God.

The angel in the centre wearing a dark reddish purple tunic with a dark blue cloak is thought to be God the Son as these colours are worn by Christ in most Icons.

The colours of the tunic symbolise both Christ's human blood and His royal status. The blue cloak signifies the mystery of Christ's divinity.

Look above the second angel and you will see a tree, signifying the Oak of Mamre in the Genesis story, but also symbolic of Christ's death on the cross.

The third angel on the right dressed in green is thought to be the Holy Spirit. Green symbolises new life, hope and renewal. Again the blue tunic draws our attention to the divinity of this person.

Over the head of the third figure is a mountain, which symbolises a spiritual journey towards salvation.

You will notice that the figures are gathered around a table. On the table lies a dish containing the meat Abraham and Sarah prepared for their guests. The dish stands at the very centre of the circular arrangement, symbolising the Eucharist, the ultimate gift, the continuing renewal of the Covenant between God and human kind.

Our place in the Circle of Life

The Trinity provides for Christians a deeply challenging focal point.

Through the loving sacrificial action of the Trinity the whole of creation, every minuscule atom, all people past, present and to come are part of this never ending circle of life – this Body – this People, this flesh and blood.

Because of this tremendous love in action, the inter- connectedness of all people, is real.

It is not just Christians who are challenged to see others as bone of their bone and flesh of their flesh – brothers and sisters, one people. This interconnectedness, this bond is an ancient as time itself. Sadly, we lost touch with those connections and have been lured into believing that we stand alone.

The Native American Peoples have long known this – so too many African tribes and Nations.

The sense of being part of something, or being able to deepen their identity, is greatly needed by the children in our classes today.

I am ...? I belong to ...? I am special because ...?

I hope that these practical ideas and suggestions will help you to deepen your own sense of belonging as well as the children.

Age Groups

You will notice that the Circle Time ideas are presented with indications for possible variations for different age groups. However, it is important to stress that each idea is flexible and can be adapted to the needs of your class.

Getting Started

Circle Time is well established in many Primary Schools and for that reason I do not propose to focus on the background or mechanics of the practice as such. For schools who are not yet using Circle Time, may I suggest that the books by Jenny Mosley might be of help.

It is very important that the class is well prepared and focused on what they are about to do before you try any of the ideas contained in this book.

Preparing the Children

Recall the class rules or charter
Recall the rules of Circle Time
Talk about the importance of this time
Remember that you are creating a special sacred space, holy ground
Talk about the importance and equality of each member of the class
Recall our common identity

> One class – sharing one life
> One school family – responsible for each other
> One people – who belong to the one human race

Talk about the importance of realising that what happens to one, happens to all
Remember what it is to be part of a community
Remember that each person in the Circle is unique and a gift to be treasured.

Ways into the Circle

When using circle time in R.E. it is important to try to raise the pupil's awareness of what is about to happen. The following are some suggestions of how this could be done.

Preparing the Space

Create a space in the room with extra care. Clean it.

Gathering the Class

Recall the story of Moses before the burning bush
Take off your shoes
Tidy yourself – you are going to enter a sacred and special place. This is holy ground

Making the Space Special

Smudging

Many Native American Nations have a special ritual for this. They call it 'Smudging'. This is a ceremony done to cleanse and purify an area, person or object. Many different herbs are used for this purpose such as: sage, which is used to cleanse, cedar to heal, sweet grass to purify.

These sacred herbs can be burned in stick form, or broken into a fireproof bowl or shell. Light the herb, fan the flame until it goes out and, using a feather, draw the smoke over the area you wish to smudge.

The sacred smoke from these herbs is used by Native Americans to communicate with the Creator and as a good way to start and end the day.

Incensing the Area

Christians are well used to the practice of using incense as a means of doing something very similar to smudging. Lighting an incense cone or stick and carrying it around the circle in a fireproof container can do this.

If you have access to a thurible this can also be used to incense the area.

Another practice is to use blessed or Holy Water. If the school does not have any blessed or Holy Water, then one of the following ideas maybe useful.

Ask if any of the pupils have Holy Water/Lourdes Water, at home. Many families do have Holy Water kept in a little bottle at home. This is something often bought back from a place of pilgrimage.

Invite your Chaplain, Vicar or local priest to come and bless some water for you. This can then be stored and used when needed.

Hold a Blessing ceremony yourselves. This can be performed by placing some water in a suitable bowl and the whole group saying a blessing over the water.

Then using an evergreen sprig, bless the area. In the same way that the incense or smudging ceremony was carried out, process the water around the special space, gently sprinkling it with water. If the pupils wish, they can dip their fingers into the water as they enter the circle and either bless themselves, or another member of the group coming behind them.

Or, if the class is recollected enough, the person blessing the space can invite each person into it by name, and bless them with water as they do so.

Aiding Participation
Soft toys, stones and shells are amongst the many beautiful artefacts used by teachers to help the children focus their thoughts and feelings during circle time and if they wish, share these with the group.

The following is an idea taken from the Navajo people in North America.

The Talking Feather

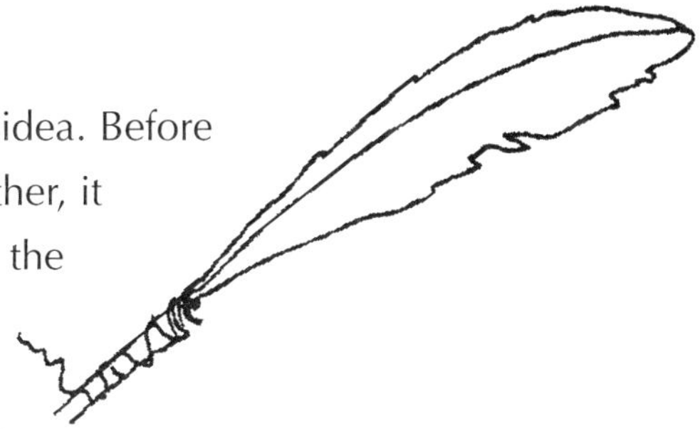

Children of all ages really respond well to this idea. Before telling them the background to the Talking Feather, it might be a good to make one yourself to show the pupils and to illustrate the symbolism and meaning.

Many cultures use the circle to express and symbolise important spiritual moments in the community's life.

When the Navajo Chief wants to hear the views of his people or bring the community to consider something of importance in their life, he calls them all into a big circle. By placing the Talking Feather in their midst, everyone knows that this was a moment of importance. Members of the circle are allowed to speak, however, once someone takes up the feather they must be very careful to only speak words of truth and honesty. To misuse the sacred circle and 'Talking Feather' is a very serious offence against the whole community and any person so doing, would be severely punished.

Why is this Feather so special?

This feather comes from the Eagle, or any other great bird sacred to the tribe. Usually one that flies the highest in their area. It is sacred because the Eagle flies high in the heavens and is born aloft by the wind, which is believed to be the breath of 'the Great Spirit'.

The breath of the Great Spirit gives life to all creation. So, when the Talking Feather is held by the speaker; their words must come as words spoken for the good of the whole community as if the Great Spirit was speaking directly to them through this person.

Decorations on the Feather

The feather is decorated with signs and designs that symbolise every aspect of the life of the community.

The feather has a tail to it with little items and 'treasures' that reflect their life. A twig, from a plant a tree that feeds them. A beautiful stone found on the river bed, feathers, or fur from other animals that sustain them, beads and decorations made from bones of animals.

Using the Talking Feather

Anyone in the circle may take up the feather to speak. Everyone in the circle must listen with an open and good heart and listening ears. They must listen for as long as the person speaks. When the speaker has finished; another may take up the feather. Or, it can be passed from person to person in the circle.

The Circle and the feather are a way of bringing the whole of time and creation together.

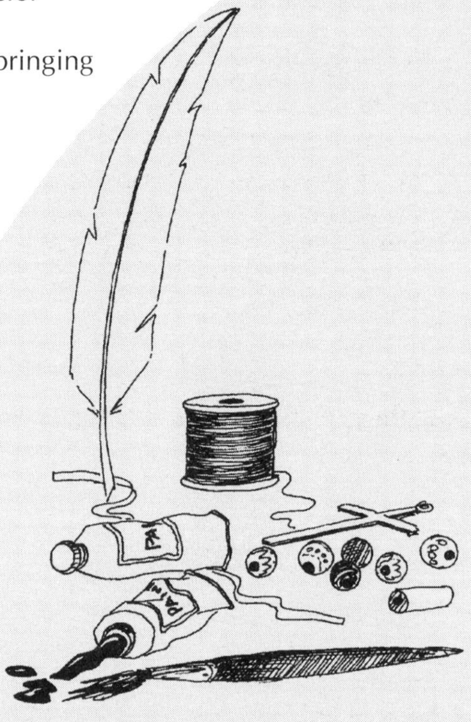

Making your Talking Feather

Suppliers:
Hobby Craft or any other craft shop
LEA resource books under Art and Craft
Internet sites

Before you embark on making a feather with your class, discuss together what they would like to put on their feather. Discuss together signs, badges, beads, items that signify something important in their life.

You will need:

a feather for each child
small strips of felt or soft material for binding the quill part of the feather
small feathers for decorating
paints
thread for binding and making 'tails'
coloured beads, little artefacts that have special meaning, e.g. Cross, medal pendant, etc.
scissors

As this activity can take some time, make sure you start it with plenty of time to finish.

Step 1
Select a feather.

Step 2
Bind the quill end of the feather with cotton thread and a small piece of felt and tie tightly. This can be a bit fiddly! This would normally be bound in leather and tied without thread. (For small children, glue the felt in place.)

Step 3
Making the tassel:

Using a strong thread, attach a bead at the end and decorate with items of significance. Simply string or tie on.

Step 4
Attaching the tassel to the feather.
Tie tightly.

Step 5
Decorating the feather.

Design on paper in rough, then either paint on directly, or glue to the feather, if this would be easier.

Looking after your Talking Feather.

A freezer bag is good for storing each child's feather. These can then be stored in a special box for Circle Time and different child's feather can be used each time by the class for a Circle Time.

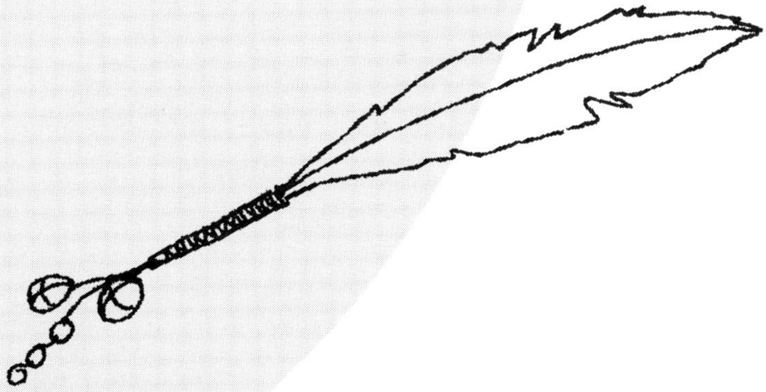

IDEA 1

Circle time ideas for the New School Year

Aim

- to develop a sense of belonging, feeling wanted, happy and appreciated
- to appreciate each one in the circle

Organisation

You will need:

name badges
a welcome card
or
a little 'Holy Card' in an unsealed envelope with a message from you naming a gift they have
or
something good about them or how happy you are to be their teacher
a green candle

Entering the Circle

If this is one of your first Circle Times with the group, but the group are used to the practice of Circle Time, establish how you are going to enter the circle and closely observe the ritual, e.g:

blessing
incense
water blessing
taking off shoes
using music

If this is the first experience for the class of Circle Time, be careful to keep the experience simple and well organised. It is better to end when the class would like to continue, than to begin with the wrong atmosphere.

Activity Focus

Place a green candle in the centre of the circle.

Step 1
Place the name badges and the unsealed envelopes of everyone in the circle around the candle. Names facing upwards.

Step 2
Light the candle.

Step 3
Welcome everyone to the circle.

Recall:

one class
one community
one body
one family
what happens to one, happens to all
all equal
all special
all priceless
all loved
all wanted
all great

Step 4
Call the name of the person sitting on your right. Go to the name badge and envelop and give it to that person. As each person does this, say:

"Welcome to your new class"

Child attaches name (do not open envelope yet).

Step 5
When everyone in the circle has received an envelope, open them together. Read silently the message. With a very young child simply look at the picture and tell them what it says, e.g:

Welcome Clare, Ian, or Mary.
Very happy to see you.
or
Welcome Danny, I want to be your friend.

(End here with younger children by singing a suitable song.)

Step 6
Invite pupils to reflect on their messages and think of how they can use them to build up the class and help everyone feel wanted and loved.

Step 7
Using appropriate object for speaking, toy, stone, feather, etc., share thoughts.

Step 8
A moment for silent reflection. Ask the circle to concentrate on the person each side of them and silently think of three good things about each of them.

Step 9
Stand, join hands, give thanks for each one by calling out each name and all saying

"Thank you Jesus for ..."
or
"We give thanks for ..."

IDEA 2

Aim
- to encourage a sense of self esteem and worth
- to help each one recognise their true beauty

Organisation
You will need:
a set of mirrors
or
one framed mirror
a green candle, sign of new life and hope. The light of the World.

Entering the Circle

Step 1
Focus the pupils through an appropriate Entry Ritual.

Step 2
Place the green candle in the centre and light it.
Explain symbolism, i.e:

Light of Christ
Green for New Life and Hope
Their new life beginning now

Step 3

Invite the pupils to close their eyes and try to 'see' themselves. Pretend they are looking at a picture – what is it like? What are they doing? Are they happy?

Children are coming up asking them to play. (*pause*)

What's happening? (*pause*)

See themselves really happy. Everyone wants to be with them.

Step 4

Open your eyes. Using their speaking object, invite the class to share what they saw, how they felt.

With young children, use one framed mirror that looks like a picture from the back. Do not let them see the mirror side. Hold the mirror up, the back towards the circle, and say. I have a very beautiful picture here – describe how beautiful using words that do not reveal that it is your face.

Invite the children to see if they know what the picture is?

Invite one at a time to come up and look at the picture.

Great exclamations – !!!

"Oh – it is such a beautiful picture."

Do this just a few times and then say – would you all like to see the picture. I will pass it around.

As each child looks – get them to say who it is.

Together say ...

And ... (name) is so beautiful.
... (name) is our special friend.

Step 5

Using a mirror, pass it around the circle inviting the class to say what kind of 'face' they want to show to the class, e.g:

When you see my face I hope you will know that I will be your friend *or*

When you see my face it will always smile at you.

or

When you see my face I hope it will always let you know that you have a friend.

IDEA 3

Hopes and dreams for the year

Aim

- to enable the class to articulate their hopes and dreams for the year ahead
- to formulate a class charter

Organisation

large sheets of paper
large felt pens
green candle
copy of the school mission statement

Entering the Circle

It may help to choose an Entry Ritual that is quite solemn to emphasise that this circle time is happy, but serious and its results are very important.

Step 1
Place the green candle in the centre of the circle, with a copy of School Mission Statement.

Step 2
Light the candle and read out the Mission Statement. (With young children, explain it in very simple terms.)

Step 3
Using the object for circle time (soft toy, stone, etc.), invite the class to say how they feel. They can live this statement in their class.

Step 4
If possible have pupils list ways in which they can live the Mission Statement on the large sheets of paper. (Scribe, if appropriate, with very young children simply share ways in which they can help to make each other happy.)

Step 5
Display all ideas. In silence reflect for a few moments. Which are the most important? Is anything missing? How can we live and work and play together in a truly loving way, in fairness, including everyone in our games – sharing and helping each other to feel loved and wanted? How can we help each other to be better each day?

Step 6
Order the main points that are agreed by the class.

Step 7
In silence, think about the areas that are most challenging. Individually, select one.

Step 8
In the circle each person is invited to say what this area is and why.

Step 9
Pass the 'talking object' around and invite offers of help, e.g:

I will help you Jenny
by ...

I will help Mark
by ...

Step 10
Join hands and silently think about these new challenges. Say together a short prayer/blessing for the whole class.

Lord, help us to be faithful to what we have just agreed
or
invite the class to write a pledge that can be recited together

Note: Make a copy for each person. Repeat it often.

IDEA 4

Using good language; words I like to hear; words I do not like to hear

Aim

- to help the pupils to appreciate the power of words
- to encourage the use and understanding of words that build one another up

Organisation

green candle
Bible with cloth, cushion or stool
2 large sheets of paper
2 large felt pens in different colours

Entering the Circle

Select an appropriate Entry Ritual.

Step 1
Light the Candle. If appropriate have a child process the candle and Bible to the centre of the circle.

Explain that the candle represents the Light of Christ.

The Bible is a very special/sacred book that tells a wonderful story. It must be handled with great care and respect as it is very different from the other books in the class. Stress that this is a Holy Book. It contains many important words.

Step 2
Place in the middle of the circle the two large sheets of paper,
one headed:

Words I like to hear GOOD HAPPY KIND GENEROUS

and the other headed:

Words I do not like to hear HURT EXCLUDED MEAN

If appropriate, use pupils to scribe or invite each child to write their words as they suggest them (with younger pupils, scribe for them).

Step 3
Spend about two minutes thinking silently about words that make us feel:

good, happy, wanted, understood
at home, loved, etc.

Step 4
Using a talking object, invite pupils to share their words and phrases. Write this on the sheet of paper.

Step 5
Now do the same with words that:

hurt, harm,
upset, exclude, destroy, etc.

Step 6
In silence, reflect on these two sheets. Share feelings, thoughts.

Step 7
Ask for suggestions about what they should do with these two lists.**Step 8**
Carry out agreed action.

Step 9
Stand and join hands. Sing together an appropriate verse or song.
Process the Bible back to its special resting place.
Recall that this book is called "The Word of God".

IDEA 5

'Good News' people

Aim

- to recognise that they are 'Good News' to identify ways in which they can be 'Good News' to one another.

Organisation

green candle and holder
Bible

Entering the Circle

Either place the candle and Bible in the circle. Invite two pupils to carry the candle and Bible placing it in the centre of the circle.

Step 1
Explain that another title for this very special Book is 'The Good News'.

Step 2
Using a speaking object, invite the pupils to say why they think the Bible is called 'The Good News'.

Step 3
Select one or two texts to be read from the Bible, e.g:

Compassion and generosity	Lk. ch6 v36-38
The call of Levi	Lk. ch5 v27-32
Jesus heals the sick	Matt. ch4 v23-24
Who is the greatest	Matt. ch18 v1-4
Forgiveness	Matt. ch18 v21-22
Little children	Matt. ch19 v13-15

Reflect silently for a few minutes.

Step 4
Invite pupils to say how they see this text to be 'Good News'.

Step 5
Explain how each person in the circle has the gift of being 'Good News' for someone else. Reflect silently for a few minutes on how they think they could be 'Good News'.

Step 6
Invite pupils to share their thoughts.

Step 7
Focus the circle back on the green candle in the centre. Light the candle. Invite pupils to silently think about each person in their class. Who do they think most needs to hear some 'Good News' today? Silently, think about this person, or pray for them. Suggest to the class that everyone tries very hard to be 'Good News' for one another.

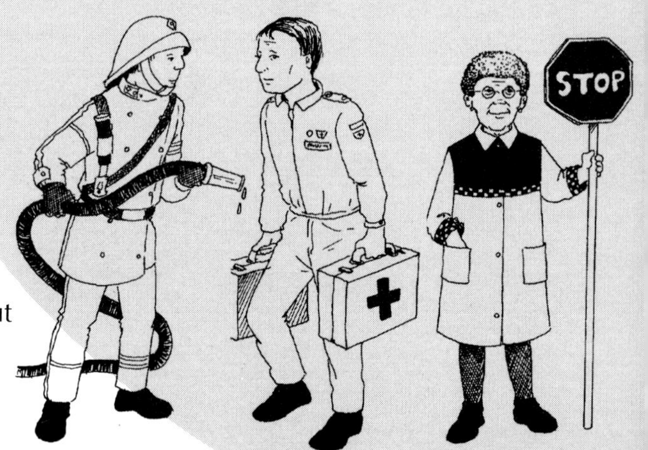

IDEAS 1-4

Aim

- to develop a sense of gratitude for the gift of life:

their life	first session
their family	second session
their friends	third session
their school	fourth session

Organisation

words of song 'Circle of Life' from the Lion King or suitable song/hymn
a white candle and holder
strips of paper in white and gold
pens
container and water for blessing

Entering the Circle

Invite the pupils to enter the circle and use a water blessing ritual, e.g. each child blesses themselves or is blessed as they enter the circle.

Step 1
Listen to the song from the Lion King 'Circle of Life'. Reflect in silence for a few moments.

Step 2
Invite the pupils to reflect for a few minutes on the words of the song. Ask them to choose the line they like the most. Read it out and if they wish, say why?

Step 3
Give each person a strip of paper and a pen. Invite them to think about what they consider to be the best thing about their life.

Step 4
Get each person to write their thoughts down. Pass the talking object and invite them to talk about what they have written, or simply place their piece of paper by the lit candle.

Step 5
Replay the song 'The Circle of Life'.

Step 6

Invite one person to gather all the paper strips into a small basket, raise them high above their heads and together say a blessing/prayer/words of thanks, e.g:

> Lord, and Creator, thank you for the gift of my life.
> Jesus, thank you for giving me my life.
> Let us give thanks for the wonderful gift of life in the greatest gift on earth.

Note

This idea may be used in many different ways. Each time you gather, it can be to focus on a different aspect of the children's lives:

their family (second session)

For this focus they can either write the names down and place them by the Candle, or bring in photos.

their friends (third session)
their school (fourth session)

With this focus invite the pupils to reflect on each aspect of their school life:

classroom
playtime
dinner time
friends
lessons

What they have learnt to do – what they want to be good at.

IDEA 5

Aim

- to recognise and develop a sense of gratitude for the gift of creation and the fruits of the earth
- to appreciate our dependence on the gifts of the earth.

Organisation

Prepare a focal point with as many natural fruits and gifts of the earth as possible:

wheat, corn on the cob, vegetables, flowers, seed, fruit, etc.

a white candle is placed in the middle
suitable music
a dish of fruit and vegetable for eating

Entering the Circle

Use a water blessing ritual to gather the class into the circle.

Step 1

Play a piece of reflective music and invite the pupils to look at the gifts of creation. Notice that each one is unique, exotic, amazing.

Step 2

Show the children the dish of food. Pass it around and invite each person to sample one piece.

Step 3

Discuss what their fruit, vegetable was like? Talk about what eating lovely food is like. Do we appreciate it? Savour it? Recognise how lucky we are to have so many gifts from the earth.

Step 4

Pass the talking object and invite the pupils to share their thoughts about the way they see food. Focus on helping the children to appreciate the vast riches of the earth and how wonderful it is to share them.

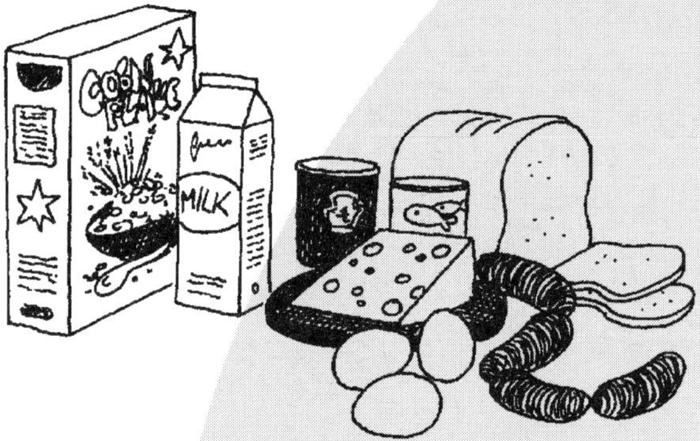

Step 5

Respect for creation. Talk about the ways in which creation is exploited, abused, taken for granted, not cared for. Share their thoughts.

Step 6

Stand and join hands around the display of the fruits of the earth. Sing a song of thanksgiving.

IDEA 1

Aim

- to enable the children to remember to celebrate people in their lives who have died
- to enable the children to understand that their loved ones are still with them but in a different form

Organisation

white candle and holder
photographs of friends and relatives, or people we know, who have died
suitable music
thirty pieces of gold A4 paper

Entering the Circle

Before entering the circle place the gold paper in the centre of the circle. Leave room for the children to sit between the gold pieces of paper.

Step 1

Enter the circle using an appropriate entry ritual. Each person carries their photos or names of their special person. Invite the children to sit between the sheets of gold paper.

Step 2

Talk about the sacredness of this circle. Today, in a special way, our remembering will remind us that our loved ones are very close to us. We carry their pictures, their names, their faces in our hands and hearts.

Step 3
Using an appropriate talking object, invite each person in the circle to call the name of their person and place the photo or name of the person on the gold paper beside them.

Step 4
Spend a few silent moments thinking and recalling these wonderful people. When the children wish, invite them to tell the circle why they are a hero or heroine, e.g. my Grandfather was a hero because he was always very kind and patient. I loved him very much.

If the children have any stories to tell about their people, encourage them to do so.

Step 5
As each person finishes speaking, place the name or picture beside the lighted candle.

Step 6
Ask the group to form a chain using the gold pieces of paper to show how we are all connected down through the ages. Sing a suitable song.

IDEA 2

Aim
- to explore ideas and feelings about life after death

Organisation

rousing music, happy, lively
a doughnut for each person (with or without a hole in the centre)
white candle and holder
tray for doughnuts
wet wipes, for sticky fingers
religious pictures of Heaven (the Internet is a good source for this).

Entering the Circle

Prepare the circle by placing the tray of doughnuts in the centre around the white candle. Play some lively, happy music.

Step 1
Enter the circle using a suitable entry ritual and place a serviette in front of each child. (Do not touch!!)

Step 2
Ask two children to give out the doughnuts and place them on the serviettes. (Do not touch!!) There will be great excitement!

Step 3
Ask the question does anyone know why they are having doughnuts. Tell the story of the doughnuts?

Ancient Irish tradition. The poor would visit the homes of the rich and offer to pray for the souls of the deceased friends and relatives. They were rewarded for their efforts with a 'soul cake', a round doughy cake, to symbolise the never ending circle of life, eternity and never ending love. With the emigration of the Irish to America this tradition of giving 'soul cakes' in payment for prayers dwindled, but the 'soul cakes' became today's doughnuts.

Step 4
Together, take one bite only from the doughnut. Enjoy it. Talk about the taste, feelings, as they eat the cake. Do they want to continue?

Step 5
Finish the cake! Wipe hands and faces.

Step 6
Play some calm music. Very simply ask the question, "Where's the doughnut gone? Is it still here?" Silently think about this.

Step 7
Using a suitable speaking object, share ideas about what they think happens when someone dies. Where do they go? What do they think heaven is like?

Step 8
Spend a few moments thinking about this silently. Show pictures of artists' impressions of heaven.

Step 9
Share thoughts and ideas. If appropriate, express ideas though artwork at a later time.

IDEA 3

Aim

- to help the pupils to recognise the importance of knowing that they too can be a hero or heroine

Organisation

white candle and holder
30 A4 sheets of white paper
pens
a packet of seeds
some quiet reflective music

Entering the Circle

Select an appropriate entry ritual.

Step 1
Give each member of the circle a small seed. Look at the seed carefully. Can they imagine what it will be?

Step 2
Using the talking object, share thoughts on what the seed contains and might become.

Step 3
Show the pupils a picture of the beautiful flower, or plant, that is contained in the seed. Ask the children to try to imagine all the things that need to happen to the seed for it to become transformed. Talk about this together.

Step 4
Explain how they, too, were this small. Now look at them! What do they think they might become? What would they like to become that would really make a difference to the world? Share their thoughts together in the circle. End here for the younger children with a suitable song.

Step 5
Give out the A4 sheets of paper and pens. Now ask the children to sit next to the person they think they know best. On their piece of paper write/draw what they think their friend really could become, that would make a difference to the world, and their reasons why.

Step 6
Share their thoughts and hopes for their friend

IDEA 1

Aim

- to help the pupils to understand and realise that they can make a difference to their lives and the lives of others
- to help the pupils know and understand the joy of putting other people first

Organisation

purple cloth
purple candles and holder
or
Advent wreath
strips of paper
pens
big sheets of paper
purple box (Change Box)

Entering the Circle

Select an appropriate entry ritual. Arrange the candle, Bible and purple cloth in the centre of the circle.

Step 1
Talk about Advent as a time for change. Putting things right that may be wrong in our lives. In these four weeks we will try each day to build ourselves up by being kind, thoughtful, understanding, patient, loving, etc. towards everyone. How do they feel about this?

Is it easy?
Is it difficult?

Step 2
Using an appropriate talking object, share their thoughts and feelings about this. Try to identify the biggest challenges.

Step 3
On the big sheet of paper, list the challenges that the class feel may face them at this moment.

Step 4
Play some quiet music and ask them to see what solution or suggestions they can come

up with for overcoming these challenges.

Step 5
Share their thoughts.

Step 6
Using the small strips of paper select one area that they feel they most need to work on. Write this down.

Step 7
Restart the music and invite each person to place their 'change' into the 'Change Box'. This now becomes their focus for the week.

Note
This idea can be repeated each week of Advent.

IDEA 2

Aim

- to help the pupils to understand that Advent is about getting ready for the birth of Jesus
- to discover ways in which they can ease unhappiness in peoples lives

Organisation

purple cloth
purple candle
or
Advent wreath
Bible
large sheets of paper with squares drawn on it
– one square for each day in Advent

Entering the Circle

Select an appropriate entry ritual. Arrange the purple cloth, candle or wreath and Bible in the centre.

Step 1
Discuss with the class why we have Advent. Why do we need such a long time? So much to do. Getting ready. A child is going to be born. What difference does a baby make to

someone's life? Using the talking object, share thoughts on this.

Step 2

Ask the children why they think Jesus was born? What was going on in the world? What difference was this baby going to make?

Step 3

Play some reflective music and ask the children to think and, if appropriate, write down all the things that they would like to change in their world today, so that it would be a better and happier place. Share these thoughts.

Step 4

Now think again, why do we have Advent?

What can we do to help ourselves?
What can we do to help our school?
What can we do to help our family?

Realise what Christmas is about, Jesus being born and that it is his Birthday. Share some thoughts.

Step 5

Take the big sheet of paper with the squares. Can we make suggestions for this week's squares? Write them in or, if there are a lot, fill them all in. Now we have a real Advent Calendar!

Step 6

Together, join hands and make a commitment to try to live each suggestion day by day.

IDEA 3

Aim

- to enable the children to see that Christmas is about Jesus' Birthday, His day
- to recognise the 'true presents' that we need to ask for at this time

Organisation

purple cloth
Poinsettia
big piece of paper
or
cut out Christmas stocking saying 'Christmas List'

Entering the Circle

Select an appropriate entry ritual. Arrange the purple cloth and Poinsettia in the centre of the circle.

Step 1
Explain to the class that the plant is called a Poinsettia and originates from Mexico. It is known there as the 'Flower of the Holy Night'. Tell them the story of how it got its name.

Long ago, on Christmas Eve, a poor boy, who had few clothes, no shoes and certainly no money, followed all the people of his village to the Church. They were very happy wearing their best clothes, specially worn for this night, during which the Christ Child was going to be born. The little boy was filled with sadness, because it was the custom of his people never to go empty handed to the Church on this night, but to take a gift that they would lay at the foot of the manager where Jesus was sleeping. He did not dare enter the Church empty handed. It was bad enough not having nice clothes, but not to bring a gift was considered very bad. He dropped to his knees outside the Church and cried, tearfully telling God how desperately he wanted to go in, but he had no gift. Thinking that he would have to return home, he got up and stared in amazement to see springing up at his very feet, a plant with dazzling red spectacular blooms. This was the answer to his prayers. Carefully, he picked the beautiful red blossoms and carried them proudly down the aisle of the Church and laid them at the feet of the Christ Child.

Step 2
Using the talking object, share thoughts about the story with the group. What was the real gift that the poor boy brought?

Step 3
Imagine that you know that you had no money for Christmas presents
and that no one could afford to buy any. How would you feel?
Share some thoughts.

Step 4
What do you think Jesus would most like us to ask for this Christmas? Share thoughts. Make a class list on a big sheet of paper.

Step 5
What do you think would make you really happy this Christmas? Do not mention material things. In silence, write a letter to the class or your family, beginning:

Dear …
This Christmas I would like to ask for the following presents:

Step 6
Christmas day is Jesus' Birthday. Ask the children to imagine what it would be like if on their birthday they were left out – people came to their party, but ignored them, didn't send them a card or present, but insisted upon YOU giving them one?

Using the talking object, share thoughts and feelings.

Step 7
Together, sing an Advent song.

IDEA 4

Aim
- to enable the children to see that Jesus is not forgotten on His Birthday
- to focus our priorities for Christmas Day

Organisation
Advent wreath
purple cloth
30 sheets of A4 paper with a day's time-table

get up
morning
lunch
tea
evening
bedtime

Entering the Circle

Select an appropriate entry ritual. Arrange the cloth and advent wreath in the centre.

Step 1
Recall together how they felt when they were getting ready to go to someone's birthday party. Share thoughts. Recall how they felt waking up on their birthday. Did they have a plan? Did they have hopes? Their feelings? Share their thoughts.

Step 2
Discuss who's birthday is on the 25th December.

Themselves?
or
Jesus?

(Allow pupils to wrestle with this idea, as it is difficult.)

Step 3
Christmas Day is for Jesus and for us. Now let's look at how we might spend the day so that we really make it the best Christmas yet. Allow pupils a free discussion and then encourage challenge. Your hopes, your families, Jesus, how do all these fit?

Step 4
Draw up a timetable of how you are going to begin your day and what you will try to do for others to make it a really happy day and thereby have a great day yourself.

Step 5
Suggest they give their timetable to their parents.

IDEA 5

Aim
- to enable the pupils to appreciate the gift of friendship and other people
- to encourage the pupils to affirm one another publicly

Organisation

purple cloth
pens
a hand bell
A4 paper designed as a scroll with someone's name.

Entering the Circle

Make a circle of chairs. Select an appropriate entry ritual. Arrange the purple cloth, candle and hand bell in the centre.

Step 1
Explain that Advent is a time for spreading 'Good News' about people.

Talk about the role of the 'Town Crier' and how he walks about the streets, yelling "Hear Ye, Hear Ye" so that everyone knows this important piece of news. Today we have Good News.

Step 2
Each pupil is given a scroll with someone else's name on it. For young children, they are given a scroll with their name on and the whole class thinks of something good to say about each one. Make this into a fun game by ringing the bell and calling:

Hear Ye ... Michael is a wonderful helper
Hear Ye ... Frances is a very lovely friend

For older pupils, let them move around the circle in any order writing something good, or something they really like, or a 'thank you', to that person.

Step 3
When everyone is finished, ring the bell and all return to their places.

A 'Town Crier' calls:

"Hear Ye, Hear Ye"

and everyone reads their scroll to themselves.

Step 4
Invite the pupils to say how they feel about what has been written.

IDEA 6

Aim
- to help the pupils to realise the importance of saying sorry and building bridges

Organisation

purple candle
or
Advent wreath
purple cloth
a bowl of water
30 sheets of A4 paper with an outline picture of a bridge.

Entering the Circle

Select a suitable entry ritual. Place the candle, cloth and bowl of water in the centre.

Step 1
Spend a few minutes reflecting with the group about the things that may still need to be worked on to make the class more united and loving towards each other.

Step 2
Using the appropriate talking object, possibly the Talking Feather, share thoughts and concerns.

When everyone who wishes has spoken, spend a few minutes working out solutions and 'bridges'.

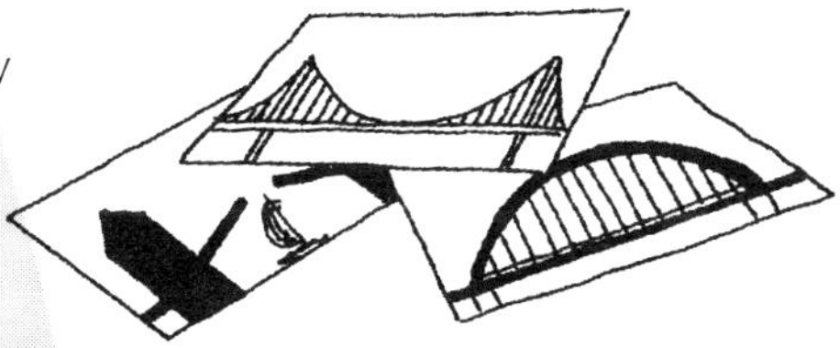

Step 3
Invite pupils to offer their ideas to the whole class.

Step 4
Give out bridge pictures. Each person writes down on the middle of the bridge what they can do to bring the group closer together, mend hurts, restore friendships.

Step 5
Invite each person to share what they have said. This then becomes a commitment.

Step 6
All stand, play some suitable music, and invite each person to come forward one at a time, put their hand in the water and bless themselves as they leave their bridge idea by the candle.

Step 7
End with the sign of peace 'Mexican Wave' style. Joining hands, you begin a gentle hand squeeze and watch it flow like a stream through the whole circle. As each person squeezes their neighbour's hand, they say "Peace be with you …" (name).

IDEA 1

Aim

- to enable the pupils to recognise and relate to Mary in the Christmas Story.

Organisation

Separate Crib figures
or
pictures of Jesus in crib/manger

use different cultural images of Mary, e.g. African or Asian
white/gold cloth

Entering the Circle

Arrange the white/gold cloth in the centre and place the figures of Mary in the centre.

Step 1
Invite the children to enter the circle either listening to a carol, piece of Christmas music or singing a Christmas song featuring Mary.

Step 2
Allow the children time to look at the images of Mary on the cloth.

Step 3
When they are ready, select one image and, using the talking object, say why they like it. What does it say to them?
or
Pass each image one at a time and invite pupils to say if this is how they picture Mary. What does this image say to them?
or
Simply pass the images and let each pupil identify their favourite and say why.

For older pupils – encourage them to say what kind of person they think Mary is.
Can they talk to her in prayer?
Is she a role model for us today?
Is she a model for boys and girls? Say why.

Step 4
End the circle time thinking about all they have heard and then quietly, in their hearts, think about the women who are very special in their lives.

Step 5
Conclude by singing a carol or song/hymn to Mary.

IDEA 2

Aim

- to enable the pupils to recognise and relate to the person of Joseph in the Christmas Story
- to recognise Joseph as a good role model for today

Organisation
Arrange in the middle of the circle figures of Joseph from various cultures if possible. Christmas card images may be useful.

white cloth
pieces of wood
paper and pens/pencils

Entering the Circle

Step 1
Using a suitable entry ritual, assemble the circle, allowing time for pupils to look at the display in the centre.

Step 2
Ask the pupils to pass the figures of Joseph around the circle.

Step 3
Invite each one to reflect on the figures of Joseph.

Step 4
When all the examples have been passed around the circle, invite pupils to share their thoughts.

Which image did they like?
Did one image seem strange?
What do they think about Joseph? (end here for younger children)

Did Joseph have a difficult
or
easy job being the foster father of Jesus? Why?
Do they think Joseph is a role model for young people today? Say why.

Step 5
When the pupils have shared all they wish to say, spend a few minutes quietly reflecting on the men in their lives:

brother
father
grandfather
uncles
cousins

Which one stands out the most, and can they say why?

Step 6
Conclude by writing a short reflection (prayer) for this person – place it by the figure of Joseph (only share it, if they so wish).

IDEA 3

Aim
- to increase the pupils understanding of Jesus as their brother

Organisation
Assemble an arrangement of crib figures of Jesus
or pictures
from Christmas cards on a white or gold cloth.

Entering the Circle

Step 1
Gather into circle using appropriate entry ritual.

Step 2
Using an appropriate talking object, talk about what has to happen to prepare for the birth of a baby:

clothes

crib/cot
room made ready
name
relatives

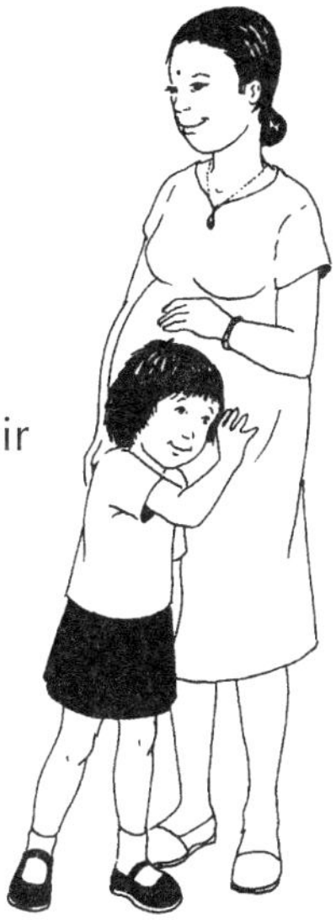

Step 3
Invite pupils to share their feelings about the arrival of a new baby in their family.
Any worries or fears? Share these using talking object.

Step 4
Talk together about the birth of Jesus:

worries his mother may have had?
worries Joseph may have had?
hopes?
what was he going to be like?
questions?
who is he?

Step 5
Using the talking object, invite the pupils to share who they feel Jesus is for them and why was it so important that he was born a tiny baby in this way.

Step 6
Conclude by listening quietly, or singing a carol that focuses on the birth of Christ our brother.

IDEA 4

Aim
- to explore with the pupils the concept of Jesus being 'the unwanted one'
- to recognise their feelings of sometimes being unwanted and how to cope with them

Organisation
Assemble a central focal point using a white or gold cloth and a variety of Christmas card pictures that show Joseph trying to find a room in Bethlehem, or the flight into Egypt.

a Bible
some stones or rocks
A3 paper and felt pens
arrange amongst the pictures to portray harsh attitudes
bowl of water
evergreen sprigs for blessing

Entering the Circle

Step 1
As each pupil enters the circle, bless the area and pupils with water
or
Tell, or read, the story of Joseph trying to find a room in Bethlehem
or
Tell, or read, the story of the Maji going to Herod to ask where they could find the new born king.

Step 2
Using a talking object, share their thoughts about how Mary and Joseph must have felt as they were continually being turned away.

How does that feel when we are 'turned away', in the playground or in the class?

Allow the pupils to give examples and encourage them to think of ways in which this could be challenged and coped with.

Step 3
Recall the story of the Magi. This is a very frightening situation.

Discuss what's going on with King Herod. His fears, feelings?

What do they think about Herod's course of action? Does this happen today?

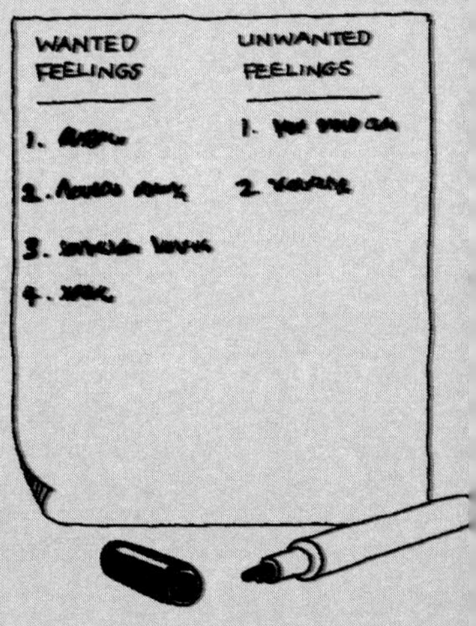

Step 4
To conclude, play some quite music. Spend a few minutes reflecting on the feelings that arise when someone feels unwanted. Say them aloud, and scribe onto each half of the A3 sheet:

Wanted feelings   Unwanted feelings

Then invite pupils to name ways in which these feelings can be transformed.

Write these in the opposite column.

IDEA 5

Aim

- to understand the story of Jesus' flight into Egypt and come to appreciate what it means to be a refugee

Organisation

arrange a focal point in the middle of the circle area
display a variety of pictures of refugees, maybe
Christmas cards, showing the flight into Egypt
a Bible
haunting music

Entering the Circle

Step 1

Play a piece of sad/haunting music as the pupils enter the circle. Spend a few minutes looking at the pictures. Read the story of the flight into Egypt, Matt. Ch2 v13-15.

Step 2

Using an appropriate talking object, share their thoughts and feelings about this story.

How would Joseph feel?
How would Mary feel?
How would they feel if this was happening to them?

Step 3

Share with the pupils the names of some of the places in the world where this is happening. Talk about why it is happening.

Step 4

Play the music again and ask the pupils to close their eyes and imagine the following:

Your parents arrive at school and say, "You leave everything and come now." They rush you to a bus ... no car ... it's gone. On the bus, your Mum/Dad tell you they are all leaving the country as fast as they can. There's a very long journey ahead. Your family have spent all their money getting tickets to go by boat to a country you've never even heard of.

You start to get upset, you haven't said goodbye

what about your toys?
what about your bike?
what about your pets?
what about your home?

(Spend a moment letting them visualise this.)

After many days of travelling by bus, no chance of a change of clothes, or a wash, little food, you arrive at a port and there's a huge old ship with thousands of people climbing on board.

you climb up the gangway
everyone is pushing
everyone is shouting
everyone is frightened

(Pause to share their feelings.) Re-enter the story:

Day after day you are tossed about on the sea. Suddenly, you hear through the loud speakers that land has been sighted.

Your Mum/Dad say to you – this will be our new home. I do hope there will be someone to help us … and then you realise:

You do not know anyone.

What comes into your mind?

your hopes?
your fears?
your feelings?

Step 6
Using the talking object, share together their hopes, fears, feelings about how they would like to be received as they get off the boat.

When everyone has shared their thoughts, play the music again and ask the children to share what they know about the 'welcome' refugees sometimes get in our country.

Conclude by making a commitment to always be ready to welcome the stranger, especially a refugee.

IDEA 6

(for the younger pupils and foundation or KS1)

Aim

- to help the pupils to understand the importance of welcoming people from far away countries and places.

Organisation

Make a focal point in the middle of the circle using:

a white or gold cloth
a collection of pictures of babies and children from different countries
a large globe or map.

Entering the Circle

Step 1

Using an appropriate entry ritual, gather the pupils into a circle.

Step 2

Show them the pictures of the children one at a time.

What do they notice about these children?

All different?
All beautiful?
All very special?

Where do they think they come from? Find places on map/globe.

Step 3

Talk about the fact that some of the children have come to this country as strangers. They have no friends.

Using the talking object, share thoughts and feelings about how they would feel if they were in this situation? (Remember, some may well have been in this situation.)

how can we show that we want them?
how can we love them?
how can we care about them?
make them part of our family?

Step 4

Conclude by singing a suitable song that stresses our love for each other, especially the stranger.

IDEA 1

Aim
- to explore ways in which they can share the 'Light of Christ'
- to help others to feel happy

Organisation
Arrange a focal point in the circle using:

a white or gold cloth
a candle
a Bible
30 pieces of A4 paper with outline of a face on it
some pens and pencils

Entering the Circle

Step 1
Sing a suitable song about light as the children enter the circle. As the pupils are singing, process the lighted candle around the circle to signify the 'Light of Christ' shining on them.

Step 2
Invite the children to look at each face in the circle.

some look happy
some look worried
some not sure
some amused

Talk together about reading faces. How do faces give a message?

Step 3
Using a suitable talking object, invite the pupils to make different faces and guess what they mean: "When I make this face, I am saying ..."

Step 4
Talk about the importance of the faces we show

happy faces
kind faces
welcoming faces
open faces
friendly faces

Step 5
How do we feel when we see faces like this?
Talk about the opposites of these 'Light faces'.
Invite the pupils to make the opposite face and guess what it means.
How do these faces make you feel?

Step 6
Conclude by singing a suitable happy faces song
or
a 'Light of Christ' song

IDEA 2

Aim

- to understand that the 'Light of Christ' can help people to see the wonderful gifts that they have been given

Organisation

a free-standing lantern with night light
a white/gold cloth
strips of paper for writing gifts
pens and pencils

Entering the Circle

Step 1
Gather the pupils into the circle using the Taizé Chant 'The Light of Christ' or another suitable piece of music.

Step 2
Invite the pupils to think of one very special gift that their neighbour has been given.

Step 3
If safe to do so, pass the lantern from pupil to pupil, inviting them to say which gift they can see in their friend.

Step 4
If the pupils are able to, they then write this down on a small slip of paper and give it to their neighbour.

Step 5
Place the lantern in the centre again. When everyone has spoken, invite each pupil to stand, and say:

> "Thank you Jesus for my gift of …
> *or*
> "Thank you Jesus for showing me one of my gifts."

Place their piece of paper beside the lantern.

With the older pupils, you may wish to extend this to include a time of reflection for the pupils to consider how they could use this gift to help bring the 'Light of Christ' to others, e.g:

> "I have been given the gift of kindness. I will try and spread this everyday to someone outside my class."

Conclude with singing "The Light of Christ has come into the world" (Taizé).

IDEAS 1-6

Aim

- to know and understand that Lent is a time of challenge and change

Organisation

The following idea can be repeated with a varied focus over the entire period of Lent. It is particularly suitable as a final activity on a Friday afternoon.

Seeing Lent as a time of challenge and change encourages the pupils to reflect on their life together and see what might need to be changed. It also helps the pupils to recognise that all actions and attitudes have an affect on others.

The following items can be used to vary the focal point. However, feel free to keep it the same, if you wish.

a purple cloth
a Bible
a cross
a broken chain – to symbolise what happens when things go wrong
a purple candle
a variety of stones or small rocks to symbolise ways in
which they may have hardened their hearts
a bowl of water
evergreen sprigs for cleansing.

Entering the Circle

Step 1

The use of the 'Talking Feather' would be appropriate for these sessions.

Explain to the pupils that they are about to review, recall, or think back over the past week. How well have they (select one area)

played together/left people out?
worked at their lessons/or not?
always done their best/or not?
used kind words/or hurtful words?
helped someone else or been selfish?
seen, and been happy about, the successes of others,
or been jealous?
given up doing something you want to do or like to
make someone else happy/or not
tried hard to help at home and respond quickly/or not?

Talk with the pupils for a few minutes about the area of review that you have selected.

Step 2
Using the Talking Feather, or any other appropriate talking object, invite the pupils to reflect on their life over the week. Remember to begin with how they feel they have tried to make progress, and where they feel that they could do better.

When everyone who wishes has shared their reflections, spend a few minutes in silence thinking about the class as a whole.

Step 3
Together, how and what can we change for the better?
Share their thoughts.
Conclude by agreeing an area and focus for the coming week.

IDEAS 1-6

(for Foundation Stage)

Aim

- to introduce the children to the practice of 'Review of Life' and help them to work together encouraging one another to grow

Organisation
Make a focal point in the centre of the circle using:

a purple cloth
a candle
a bowl of bulbs

Watch them grow each week.

Step 1
Towards the end of the week use one of the following topics to focus the pupils on the progress they have made and the areas for growth.

This week:

1 I was kind when ...
I need to try to be kind by ...

2 I tried hard to share my ...
I will try to share with everyone ...

3 I did my best work in ...
I will try hard to always to my best ...

4 I made my friends happy when I ...
I will try to make everyone happy by ...

5 I helped this week when I ...
I will try to help by ...

6 I said "thank you" when ...
I will try hard to say "thank you" when ...

Step 2
Using an appropriate talking object, invite each pupil to talk about one area of growth and then repeat this by sharing ways in which they feel they still need to try hard to grow.

Step 3
Conclude by agreeing the focus for the following week.

IDEA 1

Easter eggs

Aim

- to lead the pupils to a deeper knowledge and understanding of rebirth, new life, resurrection

Organisation

Arrange a focal point in the centre of the circle using:

a white cloth
a white or gold candle
a collection of Easter Eggs
picture of chicks hatching
picture of Christ – resurrected outside the tomb

Entering the Circle

Step 1

Gather into the circle space. Using a suitable entry ritual, either blessing with water or one person leading the class into the circle with a lighted candle.

Step 2

Look carefully at the selection of eggs. All colours shape and sizes. Talk about the symbolism of the Easter Egg.

The egg shell is hard and cold but new life will break through.

Remind the children of how chicks peck their way through the shell and crawl out into the new world. For Christians this has come to symbolise Christ's Resurrection on the third day from the tomb.

Step 3

Pass round, or hold up, a suitable picture of the Resurrected Christ.

Step 4

Pass round, or hold up, the picture of a chick breaking out of its shell.

Step 5

Using a suitable talking object, invite the pupils to say what they think and feel about the story of Christ's Resurrection. How do they think Jesus' friends felt when they saw him?

Step 6
Play some calm music very quietly. Invite the pupils to close their eyes. They are in the garden, by the tomb. What is it like?
(pause)
Now see the stone roll away
(pause)
Slowly, a person appears
(pause)
It is a man
(pause)
Can you believe what you are seeing?
(pause)
He comes up to you and you talk to each other
(longer pause)
He gives you a message …
(longer pause)

Let the music play gently.

Step 7
Invite the children to share what they 'saw' and 'heard'.

Step 8
Conclude by sharing a piece of Easter Egg with the whole class.

IDEA 2

Easter bunnies – that lay eggs!

Aim
- to enable the pupils to see the religious significance portrayed in the story of the Easter Bunny and its meaning for their lives

Organisation
Arrange a focal point in the centre of the circle using:
a white or gold cloth
a white candle

Easter Bunny
little Easter Eggs hidden around classroom or outside, weather permitting

Attach a little scripture verse to each egg with an elastic band – Jesus said "I am the resurrection and the life".

Step 1
Using a suitable talking object, gather the pupils into the circle.

Step 2
Tell the pupils the story of the Easter Bunny.

Originally, the rabbit was a religious symbol for people who were not Christians. The story comes from the legend of 'Eastre' who was the goddess of spring.

Every spring, when everything was bursting into new life, Eastre's pet bird would lay eggs in baskets and have a great fun hiding them from Eastre in her garden. Eastre would get very cross when she could not find them easily. One day she was so mad that she told her bird to show her where the eggs were hidden. When she would not Eastre changed the bird into a rabbit. The funny thing was, this legendary creature still laid eggs! So now we have an egg-laying bunny!

Step 3
Using a suitable toy, or plastic egg, pass this as the talking object. Ask the pupils to share their thoughts about the story. Do they think it was a good idea for Christians to adopt the idea of Easter Eggs?

Step 4
Hold an Easter Egg hunt. Bring your egg back to the circle and invite each person to share the message attached to the egg. What do they think it means for them today?

Step 5
Conclude by eating their Easter Eggs.

IDEA 3

Easter baskets

Aim

- to enable the pupils to recognise the true symbolism behind the Easter basket and its meaning for their lives

Organisation

Arrange a focal point in the centre of the circle using:

a white or gold cloth
a white or gold candle
a wicker basket filled with spring produce showing new life, e.g. eggs, vegetables, flowers
paper daffodils cut out for writing on
pen and pencils
a bowl of water to symbolise the spiritual significance of the new life of Easter and for blessing the produce

Step 1

Enter the circle singing an Easter Alleluia.

Step 2

Spend a few moments explaining the origins of the Easter basket and the bowl of water. Stress the point that the baskets were a thanksgiving to God for all his gifts to be shared and enjoyed.

Step 3

Give out the paper daffodil heads and invite the pupils to think of something special in their lives that they would really like to thank God for. Write this on one side of the flower.

Step 4

Using a suitable talking object, invite anyone who wishes to share their thoughts and what they would like to say thanks for?

Step 5

Invite the pupils to turn over their flower and think about the area in their lives, or of their class or families, that they would like to pray for at this Easter time, e.g: a new baby in the family

a new friend

an area that they would like to be renewed, given a new start

or changed

something in the world that needs the power and the light of the Resurrected Christ, to renew

Write this on the flower.

Step 6

Using the talking object, invite those who wish to share their thoughts.

Step 7

Conclude by placing the flowers in the basket.

IDEA 4

Easter gardens

Aim

- to help the children express their ideas about life after death through the story of Christ's Resurrection

Organisation

Use a model Easter Garden

or

create a simple one in the centre of the circle

a Bible

two small night lights placed on bricks or stones to show the Light of Christ leading out of the tomb

or

if the school/class has constructed an Easter Garden, gather around the established garden

Step 1

Gather the pupils into the circle using an appropriate entry ritual.

Step 2
For the younger pupils, tell the story of the events of Easter Morning. For the older pupils, invite them to recall the events from the moment that Mary Magdalen arrives in the garden until the point when she tells the apostles that Jesus has risen from the dead.

Step 3
Using the talking object, share their thoughts and feelings about what they think happens when someone dies.

What ideas, images do they have, knowing the story of the Resurrection about life after death.

Step 4
When everyone has spoken, invite different pupils to come forward to light the night lights.

Spend a few minutes reflecting on what has been shared.

Step 5
Conclude by singing an Easter Alleluia.

IDEA 5

Easter light

Aim
- to help the pupils understand the power they have to bring life to one another

Organisation
Make a central focal point using:

a large white candle
a white or gold cloth
cut-out letters A 'alpha' & Ω 'omega'
cut-out numbers for the year 200...
five drawing pins to represent the incense containers used for the big Paschal Candle in Church

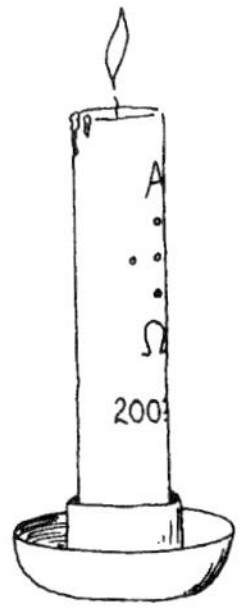

If safe to do so, give each child a small candle with a hand shield.

Step 1
Gather the pupils into the circle singing an Easter Alleluia.

Step 2
Explain the symbolism of the Easter Candle, also called, the Paschal Candle.

This great candle is signed with the Greek letters. A for alpha and Ω for omega – meaning the beginning and the end. The numbers are for the year. The five pins, with incense in, are for five wounds of Christ.

The Great Paschal Candle is lit, for the first time, very late on Holy Saturday, with the Easter Vigil being the start of the feast of Easter.

The Light of Christ has come into the world.

Step 3
Light the Paschal Candle. Invite the pupils to share why they think the candle is such an important symbol. Use a suitable talking object.

Step 4
Talk together about how they can be 'candles'

for the world
for each other
for their families

Think about candles, 'alive', giving light, giving warmth, comfort and overcoming darkness.

Step 5
When everyone who wishes to speak has done so, sing together:

'The Light of Christ has come into the World'

As they sing, one child gives out the small candles with hand protectors. One person is invited to light their candle and rejoin the circle. The light is then shared from candle to candle.

Step 6
Process back to their places singing and carrying their lit candles. Stand in their places and continue to increase the volume of the singing.

Enjoy the effect of the 'Light of Christ' moving into their classroom.

Conclude by extinguishing their candles. Point out to the pupils that although the lights have blown out, they still carry them in their hearts for all the world to see.

IDEAS 1-9

Fruits of the Holy Spirit; the Holy Spirit working in us

Aim

- to enable the pupils to recognise and know the fruits of the Holy Spirit
- to understand the power of the Holy Spirit

Organisation

The following nine fruits of the Holy Spirit are taken from the New Revised Standard version of the Bible, as this offers the simplest wording for children. In the traditional readings of Galatians ch5 v22-23 there are twelve fruits.

NRSV
Love
Joy
Peace
Patience
Kindness
Goodness
Faithfulness
Gentleness
Self-control

These Circle Time ideas all follow the same pattern but focus on a different 'Fruit of the Holy Spirit'.

For each session arrange an appropriate focal point using any of the following:

red cloth
red candle and holder
Bible
'twig tree' with each of the fruits of
the Holy Spirit handing on it in the shape
of a dove

Entering the Circle

Step 1

Assemble the pupils into a circle using an appropriate entry ritual, e.g:

singing 'Spirit of the Living God'
or
any other well known song/hymn to the Holy Spirit

Step 2
Invite the class to select the 'fruit' that they would like to focus on today.

Step 3
Using anappropriate talking object talk together about:

they need ...
the class needs ...
the world needs ...

Step 4
To conclude, agree an action that they would like to take as a class to help this fruit grow in each of them.

IDEA 10

Birthday of the Church; our birthday

Aim
- to celebrate being a community and to enjoy each other's company

Organisation
Create a focal point in the centre of the circle using:

a large birthday cake on a table cloth
30 paper plates and serviettes
30 paper cups
juice
a Bible
a red candle

Step 1
Enter the circle using a blessing ritual. Each child is blessed with water as they take their place:

Sarah, may the Lord bless you on this great

birthday of the Church
or
Michael, may God bless you with many gifts on this special day

Step 2
Explain to the pupils that this is the day that the Church officially recognises as its birthday

Step 3
Read or tell the story of Pentecost in Acts 2.

Step 4
Together, using an appropriate talking object, talk about the effect Peter and the Apostles had on the crowds.

what impact did they have?
what do they think had changed Peter?
why was he so convincing?
why did so many people listen?
how do they think everyone understood?

Step 5
Spend a few minutes reflecting on birthdays that they have had.
Why are they so special. What words describe them?
What feelings?

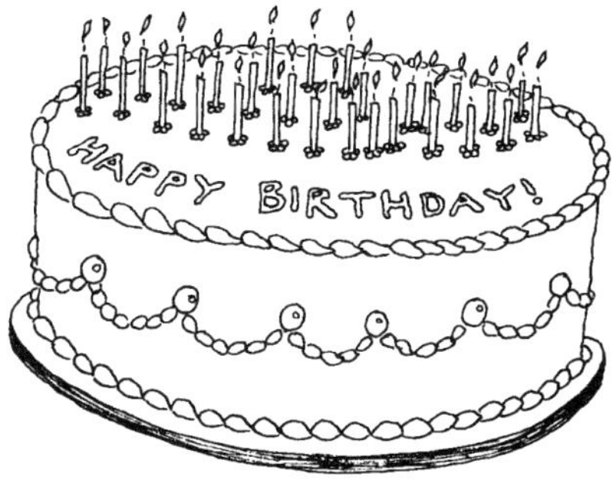

Step 6
This may be the first time that they have celebrated this special birthday. Light the candle – how old are we?

Sing 'Happy Birthday to us'.

Cut the cake and share it and pass around a fruit drink.

Step 7
After the cake has been eaten and all is finished, invite the pupils to reflect for a moment on the joy of being together.

Using the talking object, share their thoughts and feelings about what they like and enjoy about their class and say why.

Step 8
Conclude by singing a joyful song, e.g. 'Give me joy in my heart'.

IDEA 1

Mending bridges

Aim

- to help the pupils to recognise that relationships are restored and strengthened by saying sorry

Organisation

Arrange a focal point in the centre of the circle using:

a green cloth
a candle
pictures of a bridge
quiet music

Entering the Circle

Using a blessing entry ritual, gather the pupils into a circle.

Spend a few moments talking about the importance of everything that has happened over this year together. Good times, funny times, etc. Move to those moments when things have not gone so well. People in a bad mood (the teacher also in a bad mood!) and perhaps you have hurt each other. Now, before we move to the next class, or school, it is important to put things right and, if necessary, say 'sorry'.

Step 2

Using the Talking Feather, or another appropriate talking object, the teacher begins by saying that he/she is sorry if they have ...

Invite the pupils to share their thoughts and desire to say sorry. This can be kept general,
e.g. I'm sorry for the times that I have ...

Step 3

When everyone has spoken, join hands and sing 'Bind us together'.
or
any other suitable song/hymn.

Step 4

Conclude by giving the sign of peace by passing on the peace through the chain of hands, e.g. stand in a circle, all hands joined.

One person gently squeezes the hand of the person on their left and says:

"Peace be with you ..."

They then do the same to the person on their left.

IDEA 2

Memory Lane

Aim

- to celebrate ending this stage in the classes and remembering all the good things that have happened

Organisation

a green cloth
a green candle
a Bible

Before circle time begins encourage the pupils to think of a really good or funny memory from the year to share.

Entering the Circle

Step 1
Use an appropriate entry ritual to form the circle.

Step 2
Using a talking object, talk about the importance of telling stories and keeping good memories alive.

Invite each pupil to share their good and funny memories.

Step 3
When everyone has shared a story/memory join hands and sing a suitable song.

IDEA 3

Celebrating success

Aim

- to enable the pupils to recognise their many achievements during the year and celebrate them

Organisation

Before this Circle Time, ask the pupils to select one or two pieces of work that they feel are their very best achievements.

Arrange a focal point using:

a green cloth
a green candle
a Bible

Entering the Circle

Step 1

Gather the pupils into the circle using one of the blessing rituals.

Step 2

Using an appropriate talking object, invite the pupils to share their achievements and say why they are pleased with them. As each person finishes, they place their work around the focal point.

Step 3

Spend a few moments in silence thinking about all the achievements that have been shared.

Step 4

Conclude by singing a 'Thank you' song.

IDEA 4

I want to thank you for ...

Aim

- to offer the pupils the opportunity of saying

'thank you' and being affirmed themselves

Organisation
The circle is made up of chairs, one for each person.

Place on each chair, pens and a piece of paper headed:

Name ... I want to thank you for ...

gentle music

Entering the Circle

Step 1
The pupils are invited to enter the circle and sit in front of the chair with the piece of paper with their name on.

Step 2
Explain that they are going to move to any chair they wish to kneel in front of it and write a 'thank you' to that person.

Step 3
When everyone has written on each paper, return to their own chairs and sit in front. Quietly, whilst the music is playing, read your own 'thank you' page.

Step 4
Using an appropriate talking object, invite all the pupils to share their thoughts.

Step 5
Conclude by joining hands in a circle and singing a friendship or thank you song.